WHAT DOES SUCCESS LOOK LIKE?

Turning Your Goals And Dreams
Into Action Plans That Work

By

VANCE WITHERS

Copyright © Vance Withers 2021
This book is sold subject to the condition that it shall not, by way of trade or otherwise, be lent, resold, hired out, or otherwise circulated without the publisher's prior consent in any form of binding or cover other than that in which it is published and without a similar condition including this condition being imposed on the subsequent publisher.
The moral right of Vance Withers has been asserted.
© 496 Kitchen – part of the 496 Partnership
ISBN: 9798745359415

MAKING PEOPLE COUNT

DEDICATION

To my wife Karen and to my children Jamie, Elliot and Hannah for their love and always being there to support me.

CONTENTS

ACKNOWLEDGMENTS I

INTRODUCTION 1

BACKGROUND TO THE BOOK 7

WHO'S THE BOOK FOR? 30

PREPARING YOURSELF 37

STEPPING OUTSIDE OF YOUR COMFORT ZONE 51

THINKING DIFFERENTLY – CREATING THE GOAL 66

POTENTIAL AREAS TO CONSIDER 81

CREATING YOUR PLAN 106

WORKING THROUGH THE PROCESS 115

DETAILING SPECIFIC ACTIONS 129

MONITORING AND MEASURING PROGRESS.............. 132

ENJOYING SUCCESS 139

USEFUL TOOLS... 142

ABOUT THE AUTHOR 146

ACKNOWLEDGMENTS

To my first manager for supporting and believing in me and to the colleagues, clients and customers with whom I've shared so many learnings and wonderful adventures.

"Twenty years from now you will be more disappointed by the things you didn't do than by the ones you did do."

- Mark Twain

Introduction

WHAT DOES SUCCESS LOOK LIKE?

How many of you have been asked that question? How many of you have asked yourselves that question? How many of you have a dream or a vision of the future that keeps coming back to you but are afraid to take the first steps to achieving your goals, your ambitions, or your dreams? Have you ever wondered what gets in the way of individuals achieving their goals or companies that never quite manage to get to the next level?

The question of what the future might hold is one that's frequently asked by many people in many different situations. However, it's a question that's usually not fully answered. In commercial life, it's a question which is often asked on a weekly, if not daily basis.

Whilst it may not have been a question that we asked ourselves in the past, the Covid-19 pandemic has changed the outlook of so many people and it's a question that more and more people are now asking themselves. The Covid crisis forced unprecedented change across the globe and caused huge numbers of people to review what they're doing with their lives and start questioning why they're doing what they're doing. I don't believe that there is ever a bad time to start to think about what we have, where we are, and what could be. It's healthy to think (some would say to dream) about doing different things or doing things differently, maybe even doing better things. Covid-19 has shown us how plans and goals can be shattered in an instant and our everyday realities become unrecognisable. However, that doesn't mean that we should stop making plans. Far from it in fact. It may simply be that we have to review our expectations on how long something will take or we might have to think about doing different things in order to achieve what we want to.

For many people, the whole concept of the question could now be even more daunting that it remains just a dream. Any thoughts that they might have had will stay firmly in the 'what if' box. It's all too easy to look at other people, make comparisons and dismiss your own situation with a simple phrase like, "I could never do that" or "It's alright for them but…" The truth is that for all of us, although our vision of what success looks like will be personal and potentially very different from anyone else's, it doesn't make it any less valid or worthy.

The media today is full of images of people who claim to be amazingly successful and make promises that they can recreate this success and fantasy life for you. We have to make our own judgements as to how 'successful' they are but, in reality, we're only judging one dimension of the whole scenario. There are no 'get-rich-quick' schemes. They may appear to have the trappings of wealth, but do they have a happy family life? Are they healthy? They may have thousands of followers, but can they hold a simple conversation with another human being? The world seems to be full of 'experts' who promise you amazing results by simply signing up to their programme. There's no discussion with you to see if it's the right choice for you, they just want your money and time.

Indeed, for some people success is simply measured by the amount of money in the bank that they have whilst for others it can be the amount of time that they have to spend with their family or friends. Whatever your vision of success might be, I want to share with you a simple way to approach this question which will work whoever you are and whatever your circumstances are. It's certainly not my place to give you any pre-defined lists or examples of what success looks like. It's entirely up to you to decide what your goals are. What I do have is a process, a 'template' that will help you capture what success means for you and allow you to start to build your plan on how to achieve that success.

For myself, the year 2020 started well and the outlook seemed promising. Then just as things were falling into place, Covid-19 came along and changed everything. Clients were furloughing staff, virtual meetings became the new norm, and we seemed very distant from each other. In reality, the connection technologies and tools that had been around for a while suddenly came into their own and having conversations and meetings via video link became 'just the way we did things'.

In fact, for many people the restrictions on travel and the elimination of face-to-face meetings brought them much closer to some people and brought more focused dialogue to almost every conversation.

In my own world, with people facing so much uncertainty, I chose to put my own ambitions on hold and to focus on helping others through the crisis. Whether that was through delivering food and medicines to those less fortunate in the community or simply by being there to listen to people's concerns. I wanted to be a voice of calm in a sea of trouble. My focus switched to others and how they might get through this. These were uncertain times. No one knew what would happen next. It just seemed wrong to push my own agenda and vision of the future when people weren't able to think past the next day.

My long-term plans didn't change – my speed, my focus, and my methods had to change to reflect what was going on.

Things do change and everyone's expectations are different. We need to ignore stereotypical visions of success and avoid focusing on the visions and values of others. We should not judge our own success against the success of others. We need to create space for alternatives – your alternatives. This is **your** journey and it's critical that you decide for yourself.

"If you can dream it,
you can achieve it."

– Zig Ziglar

Background to the book

In my previous book, "Cooking for Business", I set out to share what I have found to be the common views on what the key 'ingredients' for success are in a number of areas of commercial life. Having a recipe to follow is often the best way to move forward and feel confident in the knowledge that you're following a similar path to others before you. It's also reassuring that you're using tried and tested 'ingredients' to help you deliver sustainable success and outstanding results.

But what if you don't have a recipe to follow? What if the 'ingredients' are not defined for you? What if the choices were all yours to make? This can be daunting for many people and can often prevent them taking the first steps towards realising their dreams or lifelong ambitions. Without a recipe to follow, we need a different approach.

What I'm sharing with you is an approach that I took when I was personally at a very low point in my life. My 'dream' job had been taken away from me and I struggled to find meaning in what I was doing. I took another role but somehow it didn't seem enough. I realised that I had to create my own version of the future and follow that path.

Based on the approach that I took back then, I've set out to create a book that would stimulate thinking and provide practical suggestions and simple tools that can be easily used by anyone. It's about thinking positively, thinking precisely, and taking action. As I said earlier, this is not a 'get-rich-quick' process and there are certainly no guaranteed results. What I can guarantee, however, is that once you've invested the time to identify what success looks like for you clearly and precisely, developing the plans to get you started on that journey will be much easier and it will becomes easier to communicate and explain those plans to people who might share that journey with you. It's critical to understand that being able to fully explain what you want to achieve or how you want to achieve something will affect the level of support that you can generate and the level of success that you can achieve. Having clarity and shared ownership with family, friends, or colleagues is one of the key factors in determining the success that you'll be able to achieve.

As I said previously, this book is about taking action. It's critical to recognise what you can control, what you can influence and what you can do nothing about. It's about getting you to focus your energies where you can make a difference – not wasting your energy concerning yourself with things that you can't change. Consider the lists that follow. They don't contain everything, but they contain enough to make you realise just how much is actually under your direct control or influence.

We often assume that we can do nothing when in reality we can change outcomes in a great many areas. It's a question of attitude. As Henry Ford once said – "If you think you can or you think you can't, you're right." Our attitude determines our willingness and ability to take action.

This book is about achieving success. Success for you and those people around you – on your terms and in your own time.

Take a moment to consider those things in your life that you can actually control and those things that, even though you can't control them, you can influence them through your actions.

Things that you cannot control

World events

Your natural height

Who your parents are

Your natural skin colour

Other people's general attitudes

The weather

Commodity prices

Exchange rates Interest rates

What other people read

Past events

What other people do in private

What the media say

Things that you can influence

Other people's moods

How other people treat you

How other people behave

How your family treat you

How people speak to you

People's attitudes towards you

People's respect for you

Your children's behaviour

Deadlines that are given to you

How other people handle their responsibilities

How much effort another person puts into something

Things that you can control

Your emotions

Your effort

Your energy

Your focus

Your fitness

Deadlines that you set

Your interests

Your time-keeping

Your respect for others

Your circle of friends

How hard you work

Your knowledge

Your weight

Your skills

The amount of help that you give to others

The amount of effort that you put into something

Your behaviour

What media you read

Your level of interaction with other people

How you treat your family

How you display your feelings

The amount of time that you spend in the office

How you speak to other people

What and when you eat

What you drink

How much you read

How you react to challenges

Your mode of travel

Your humility

Your kindness to others

How much you give to charity

How you handle responsibilities

How much help you ask for

Your manners

Your mood

Your perspective on life

The people you trust

It's often a shock to people to realise how much that falls directly under their control. Of course, the list could be longer and I'm sure you're already thinking of your own situation, but the key is to realise just what you can actually achieve with what you have at your disposal. Making the most of your thoughts, your actions, your attitude and your beliefs and values is what will help you to achieve the success that you strive for.

As the Covid-19 crisis so clearly showed us, it's pointless letting yourself be discouraged by things that you can do nothing about. Focus your efforts where you can make a difference and certainly don't waste your energies in areas where you can make no difference at all. That will only lead to isolation, frustration, and potentially to bitterness.

"You cannot control what happens to you, but you can control your attitude towards what happens to you, and in that you will be mastering change rather than allowing it to master you."

- Brian Tracy

PERSPECTIVE

I mentioned perspective as one of the elements that you can control in your own life – how you see things, what you feel about them, and what you do about them.

Of course, things do appear differently to us the closer that we are to them. That's only natural. Something will appear larger to us the closer that we stand to it and a world event will affect us differently depending on how 'close' we are to the subject. For example, stories of redundancies taking place have a greater impact on us if we too have been made redundant. We understand first-hand what people are going through. As a keen artist, I was (and still am) frustrated when individuals fail to pay proper attention to perspective when they sketch or paint objects. To me it's so simple – apparently to others it's not!

In art, as in life, you have to apply the correct perspective to have the greatest impact. Being able to put things into context and not to get over-stressed about any given situation is something that we should always try to do. Why get stressed about things that we cannot control?

"Everything we hear is an opinion, not a fact.

Everything we see is perspective, not the truth."

- Marcus Aurelius

MY PERSONAL BELIEFS AND VALUES

My beliefs and values provide the perspective with which I view life and events within my life. I wasn't born with these values, they were influenced by people around me, what I've experienced, and what I have learned over time.

To put things in context, I've spent a large amount of my life in corporate roles, working for and alongside some really great people. That experience shaped what I believe to be the critical beliefs that influence and, to some degree, protect my life. Over the years some may have changed, and most have been 'updated', but the core remains constant.

I've listed below my personal beliefs/values and the principles by which I live every day – what I deem to be a successful way of managing my day-to-day life. I haven't done this to try to influence you. I've done it to encourage you to make the time to identify or realise for yourself the values and principles that influence you on a daily basis.

"When your values are clear to you, your making decisions becomes easier."

- Roy Disney

My values are as follows:

1. I judge myself by my own achievements, not someone else's
2. I keep close with my immediate family
3. I make time to stay in touch with friends
4. I work hard and will always put the hours in that are required
5. I will always make time for me, my family, and my interests
6. I strive to always be on time and if I can't be on time, be early
7. Being late never has never been acceptable and never will be
8. I invest time in those things that I feel passionately about
9. I don't try or claim to know everything
10. I stop doing things that I don't enjoy
11. I always have a plan but like to take one step at a time
12. I eat sensibly but I am not obsessive
13. I hold firm views but won't force them on others
14. I will always listen before speaking and I give my opinion when asked
15. I believe that wisdom is more important than knowledge
16. I have always and will always respected authority
17. I don't feel bad because I can't support every charity
18. I will do whatever I can for someone who has less than me
19. I strive to do the right things AND to do them right!
20. I am always open to new ideas

As I said earlier, I share these not to influence you but to give a different perspective and far from limiting my outlook on life, my beliefs have always allowed me the space to explore new ways of thinking, to find new ways of looking at things and to try new experiences. You may not agree with all of them and will certainly hold some firm beliefs of your own, but my beliefs have allowed me to make the choices that were right for me. Of course, I've made mistakes along the way, but I know that I've taken the time to look at new things and whatever the outcome, I've gained something from the experience. Having a clear plan has always helped me to know where things might have gone wrong and through that, I've discovered what my own strengths and limitations are.

Like me, I'm sure that you've built up a close network of individuals whose opinions you respect and trust and it's always good to get their input. When it comes to deciding what success looks like for you, it's better for you to sit alone and develop your own thoughts. Depending on who you share your thoughts with, you'll hopefully get input to help you to plan to achieve your goals rather than give feedback that directly challenges the wisdom of your choices and of your thinking. Staying true to your values will give reassurance to those around you and will add credibility to your thinking.

"One person with a belief is equal to a force of ninety-nine who have only interest."

- John Stewart Mil

SUCCESS IS A PERSONAL THING

If you have ever suffered a disappointment, there will probably have been people close to you who were quick to offer you advice. Some are well-meaning, some just want to say "I told you so" but it's almost always advice that's based on their own perspective, not necessarily their own experience. Whilst I would suggest that you listen to feedback, it's important to view any advice that you receive with the caution it deserves. What I view as my success may not seem like success to some others, but it is to me and that's what matters. The same will be true for you. Too often we are too heavily influenced by media images or other people's definitions of success. Putting feedback into perspective is a vital part of any successful project.

Your view of success is personal to you. It always has been and should always be. Of course, you can be influenced by what you see around you, but you should not 'slavishly' follow someone else's plan in the hope that you find whatever it is that you're looking for.

All my experiences so far in life don't mean that I'm content with where I am or what I've achieved and neither do they mean that I'm unhappy with where I find myself. I am one of life's eternal optimists – there is always a way to do something and always a solution, even in the most difficult of situations. The trick is to find the time to find it!

In commercial life, we're given a very clear vision of what success looks like for the business, but usually this stands on its own and often will only be achieved at the expense of the individuals working to deliver that vision.

This book is about doing what is right for you. Be bold and you will achieve more. Don't let the chance of failure limit your confidence and your appetite in setting goals but remember that you must remain realistic.

For example, if you've never run a marathon, you could just turn up one day and try to run 26.2 miles but, realistically, it's unlikely that you'll put in a great performance. You may not even make to the end! In reality, most people can't expect to run a marathon without training for it, but if you really want to, you can do so. Really wanting to do something is the key and common sense says that you must train. How much training you are able do will dictate how long it takes to get yourself fit and prepared to run the marathon. But run it you will.

Encourage goal setting with the rest of your family, but don't force it. Let your children express what they want to do in the way that they want to do it. Encourage thinking outside of the norm. If you're scared of risk, take steps to minimise it. You may even want to take an entirely different career path to the one that you're on, but if you have financial considerations (as so many of us have), you can't just stop one job on the Friday and expect to start running in your new venture on the Monday. Things take time and you need to plan the transition.

We should never be 'doing' without 'thinking', but never let your 'thinking' get in the way of 'doing' something. Just thinking about something achieves nothing but considering options, being realistic, planning contingencies, and taking action does.

If your goal is to achieve a meaningful work-life

balance, share that with your employer. For some people the work-life balance means working from home and for some it means working for themselves. It could be enough for you to be able to work flexible hours, but you still need to define what success looks like. If you choose to work from home, the temptation to 'just do an hour's work' is immense because it is literally on the doorstep. Discipline is the key. Decide how you want to work and share those disciplines with those around you. Just because dad or mum is at home does not mean that they are not working. The truth is that they are trying to work more effectively and need space to do so.

"Don't confuse having a career with having a life."

- Hillary Clinton

HOW CAN YOU USE THIS BOOK?

What point is there in having a great vision if people do not know what they have to do to achieve or deliver it? How frustrated do you get when people 'do it differently' to how you wanted it done? The answer has to be in the way in which you communicated the task. Did you clarify what you wanted or expected? The probable answer is 'no' and so what could you have done differently?

The reason that many business initiatives fail is not because they were the wrong thing to do, far from it. It's because they were poorly communicated. No one knew enough about what was expected. No one was motivated to do different things as not only were they unable to see the bigger picture, they found it difficult to appreciate how all the different elements affected the overall success of the project. It's great to be a charismatic leader but if you can't communicate your 'vision' to others, your success will be limited.

The good news is that there is a way to successfully communicate your vision to the rest of the team or to an even wider audience. A process that allows you to spell out what is needed to deliver the vision and avoid any misunderstandings.

Using the 'What Does Success Look Like?' process and tools will enable you to do just that. It will allow you to explain precisely what it is that you're looking for. You'll enable people not only to 'see' the goal but also to 'feel' it. If you want people to be better, tell them what better looks like and agree where they are and agree how you bridge the gap. If you want your business to be better, tell everyone what better looks like. Do not allow ambiguity to exist.

I wonder how many personal dreams, change programmes, and initiatives don't come to fruition because the outcomes haven't been clearly defined, and the precise actions required haven't been clearly detailed. How will you ever succeed if you haven't defined what success is and those around you don't know what the 'end game' is supposed to look like? If no one actually shares or even understands your vision, it will be difficult to get the results that you're looking for.

It's essential to take simple steps:

1. Define what you want
2. Understand where you are
3. Plan the transition
4. Set milestones
5. Monitor progress
6. Review success

Of course, these principles will apply in normal family life as much as they do in a business environment. Some people find it easy to speak to their family about what they want to achieve but some people find it quite difficult. In some families, the views of different generations can be at odds with each other with one group preferring a tried, trusted, and traditional approach, whilst another group may be ready to cast tradition aside and try something new and bold. The truth is that even the most conservative individuals can be convinced of at least considering a different approach if they're presented with a simple, easy to understand plan, with realistic ambitions. Simple, easy steps that allow progress without significant risk.

The trick is to get started.

"The secret of getting ahead is getting started. The secret of getting started is breaking your complex, overwhelming tasks into small manageable tasks, and then starting on the first one."

- Mark Twain

Who's the book for?

The book is for anyone who wants to take a fresh look at any aspect of their lives – work, play, family, friends, career, hobbies, interests, education. You don't have to be in a corporate environment to get the benefits from following a process. You don't have to stick with what you've got just because you don't have the framework to help you think about how different things could be.

Some of the typical applications/situations where the processes in this book can help are:

- Changing jobs
- Moving to a new house
- Losing weight
- Managing relationships

- Taking your business to the next level
- Building a high-performing team
- Managing customers
- Developing new business
- Using your time more effectively

The simplicity of the process means that not only can it be used in the situations above, it can be used for other important things like planning your retirement, planning a family wedding, or even working on your own key relationships. The process can also be used for more 'straightforward' tasks such as redesigning your garden, redecorating your house, or setting up a 'home office'.

The key steps of being clear about what it is you're trying to achieve and then breaking that goal down into 'bite size', specific pieces has potential in all walks of life. Bringing clarity to a subject means that you can actually see and share what you're trying to achieve. It pays to be bold in your thinking and in your choices, maybe even courageous, but above all, be clear about what it is that you want to achieve and what you need to do to achieve it.

What the book contains

Contained within the book are ideas, tools, and techniques that you can use to help you take a fresh look at the challenges that you face, to see them from a different perspective and to approach situations with a far more open mind.

You may find it useful to use the template or you may prefer to use your own approach. It doesn't matter what approach you take – the key is to make sure that you get started and allow yourself the opportunity to explore what opportunities might exist.

The beauty of what we're trying to do is that there are no right or wrong solutions and certainly no right or wrong ways to do things. Only you can decide how you approach things and how much commitment you'll give to it. Whatever you choose, it's important to think things through carefully and to 'test' your thinking before launching into any new initiatives.

If you have too many options and ideas, you'll be 'blinded' by the choices that you have and it's unlikely that you'll be able to get started on any of them. Be sure to prioritise your thoughts and ideas. Each one might be an absolute 'winner', but you can't do everything! Start with a broad view and then spend time to re-focus. Having less to focus on means everything will get much more attention.

"The journey of a thousand miles begins with one step."

- Lao Tzu

WHERE THE CHALLENGES COULD ARISE

One of the first things that you notice when you start to share new ideas and plans with other people is just how 'negative' or 'sceptical' they can be. Certainly, they think that they're being helpful, but they are seeing everything through their own eyes, with their perspective applied. They need to take time to understand what's driving you and your actions. They will more than likely advise you to focus on what you're doing now and try to convince you not to 'daydream'. They'll say things like: "that sounds like a great idea but…." Or they'll say: "good idea – why don't we look at that when we get a break in the schedule". Some of these things can sound initially encouraging, but they're all designed to put you off, to limit your enthusiasm, and to discourage you from taking any risk.

Remember, you're sharing information to inform other people, not to seek permission!

If the first feedback that you receive is challenging or negative, you'll start to have doubts. It's only natural that you do. This is why it's so important to be as specific and realistic in your thinking as you can be. Having clarity in your thinking will help you to 'deflect' doubt and negative comments.

To dream is perfectly acceptable but being realistic is critical because you have to recognise the constraints that you may be under. For example, the time it might take to do something, especially when you're attempting it from a standing start. Be careful not to change your overall goal, just change how you get there. Take a different route, take smaller steps and achieve them more easily. Success will bring momentum, energy, and motivation and will certainly lead to further success.

You will be challenged, that's a fact. Managing the amount of challenge is something that you must consider. Your plans must be specific, your goal must feel attainable and it must be easy for anyone involved to understand exactly what's needed from them to make it happen.

Without a plan there will be limited enthusiasm outside of your own motivation. Without clarity, progress will be slow and difficult to track. Without focus and attention, the energy and momentum will not sustain itself.

"Challenges are gifts that force us to search for a new centre of gravity. Don't fight them. Just find a new way to stand."

- Oprah Winfrey

Preparing Yourself

HOW TO PREPARE YOURSELF

Set time aside when you know that you can ensure that there will be no disturbances. Manage your diary – if you can't manage your diary to find the time to do this, then you'll never find the time to complete the tasks that you need to. It's not what you write down that matters – it's what you do that counts! If need be, do it at weekends when the business phone is switched off or you'll be receiving a lot less calls.

Think of things that make you feel good and surround yourself with those things if you can – a favourite photograph or picture for example. Move to a space that makes you feel relaxed and 'open' to new ideas. Take a walk, get some fresh air, and do whatever you can to free your mind from the usual day-to-day thinking.

These sessions are best conducted on your own, away from distraction. If you want or need help, ask someone to join you if you value their 'constructive' input and you know that they will prompt you to think broadly. Avoid those individuals who only see the reason why not to do something. They'll tell you that they're only trying to help but in reality they can be a destructive influence that you don't need when you're at this early stage of the process.

Think big.

Think positively.

Be bold.

Remember, 'why not' is a question **not** an answer.

What's driving you?

It's important to identify and to understand what your personal motivation is. It's vital that you're not chasing someone else's dream but you're focusing on achieving yours.

All of us are driven by different things and we're driven by different things at different times in our lives. What motivated you when you were in your twenties and thirties is probably not the same that motivates you if you're in your fifties or sixties. Things change over time and are influenced by what's going on around you and to you at work, at home, in your relationships, and so on. There are no right and wrong answers – just the answers that are relevant to you.

For some people, working for themselves is all that they want to do. They want the freedom and flexibility that comes with 'being your own boss'. For other people, the routine and reassurance that working for someone else brings is all that they desire.

So, how can you understand what's really driving you? You can guess and you could ask other people, but you need to find a way of assessing different motivational factors in such a way as to build a clear picture of what your primary drivers are. It will give you the confidence to leave out or include certain elements in your plans

Some people are entirely driven by money. They don't mind what job they do as long as it provides them with the level of renumeration that they need to manage and enjoy their lives in the ways in which they choose to. For other people it's about the work that they do, the people they work with, and perhaps the level of recognition that they get for doing a 'good job'. Rest assured that whatever drives you will be different from that of other people and it will certainly be different for you than it once was – and it will change again at some point in your life.

Examples of what motivates you could be:

Having a number of trusted friends

Belonging to a group or society

Having a job with prospects

Spending time with your family

Spending time with your friends

Taking regular holidays

Staying fit

Eating out

Having a job close to home

Being able to work flexible hours

Trying new experiences

Having a well-paid job

To help you take a 'snapshot' of where you are with your own personal motivation, we'll use a system of 'paired comparison'. This means that we'll compare each motivational factor with every other motivational factor in a way which will prove us with a clear overview of what our priorities are.

For example, if we look at the list above, would it be more important to you to have a job with prospects or to have a job close to home? Would it be more important to you to have a job with prospects rather than being able to work flexible hours? I'm sure that you get the idea behind the process. Once you've completed the exercise for all motivational factors, you simply count up the number of times that each element has appeared and the ones that have appeared the most times are your priorities.

It's essential when you do this to remain completely honest with yourself. Do not try to answer it in order to produce a specific result. Only by being honest will you get a valid output and only with a valid output will you be able to start to build a plan that will work for you.

Using the grid over leaf, you simply insert the number that corresponds to each motivational factor in the box underneath every other motivational factor.

For example, if having a well-paid job is more important than having a trusted friend, then you enter '1' in the box in the column headed 'Trusted friends'.

If having a well-paid job is less important to you than having a job with prospects, you enter a '3' in the box in the column headed 'A job with prospects'

I've indicated this in the diagram:

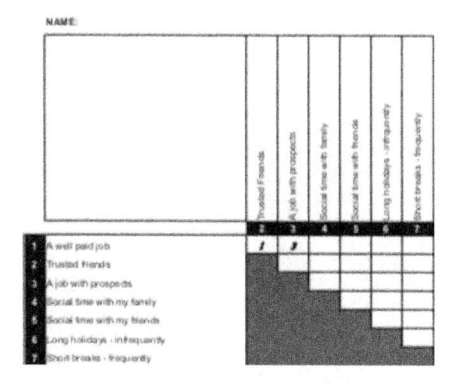

NAME:

		Trusted Friends	A job with prospects	Social time with family	Social time with friends	Long holidays - infrequently	Short breaks - frequently
		2	3	4	5	6	7
1	A well paid job	1	3					
2	Trusted friends						
3	A job with prospects					
4	Social time with my family				
5	Social time with my friends			
6	Long holidays - infrequently		
7	Short breaks - frequently	

NAME: _____ **DATE:** _____

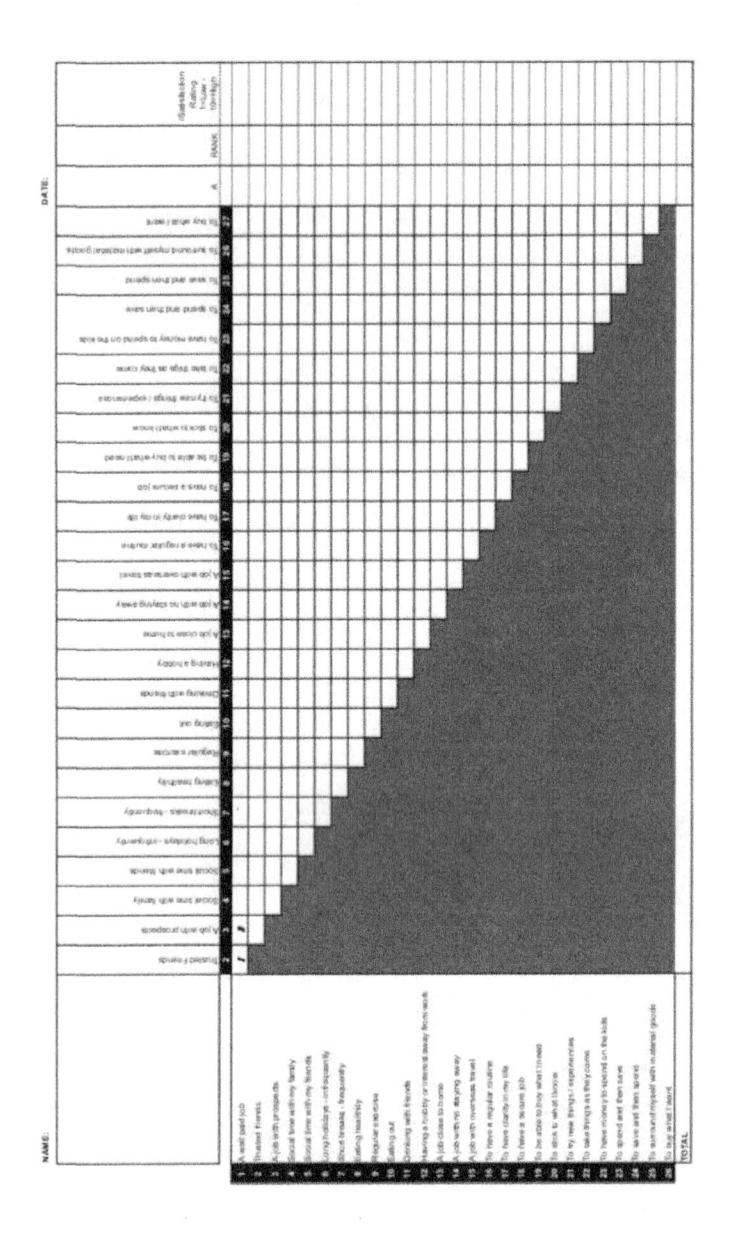

1	Trusted Friends
2	A job with prospects
3	Social time with family
4	Social time with friends
5	Long holidays - infrequently
6	Short breaks - frequently
7	Eating healthily
8	Regular exercise
9	Eating out
10	Drinking with friends
11	Having a hobby
12	A job close to home
13	A job with no staying away
14	A job with overseas travel
15	To have a regular routine
16	To have clarity in my life
17	To have a secure job
18	To be able to buy what I need
19	To stick to what I know
20	To try new things / experiences
21	To take things as they come
22	To have money to spend on the kids
23	To spend and then spend
24	To save and then spend
25	To surround myself with material goods
26	To buy what I want

TOTAL

Columns: A | RANK | Satisfaction Rating 1=Low 10=High

Once completed, the grid will either confirm what you have known for some time or it will provide you with a set of conclusions that challenge your thinking. Either way, the results will provide you with a checklist to ensure that whatever you do or whatever your plans are, your personal motivation requirements will be matched by what you undertake and achieve. Once you realise that and you see the success start to build, your overall motivation increases and success will be ever easier to attain.

Remember, you're doing this for you and how you will feel, not for others and how you might look.

"The only way to do great work is to love what you do. If you haven't found it yet, keep looking. Don't settle."

- Steve Jobs

DON'T DWELL ON THE POTENTIAL PITFALLS

There is definitely a school of thought to say that you must have a 'Plan B', something to turn to if your original plan goes off course. The problem with this is that you have to devote a great deal of your thinking to imagining that things won't work. The challenge with human beings is that we're naturally in tune with our negative side, our doubting side, and we'll often place more credence behind the potential problems than the potential successes.

Challenge every question of 'But what if it doesn't work?' with the opposite question of 'But what if it does work?'

Let's worry about things that go wrong **WHEN** and **IF** they go wrong – let's not spend time worrying about things that might not happen. If you can think about them now, you can certainly think about them when they happen – don't waste time on unproductive things.

It's critical that once you've identified where the challenges might be, you must not dwell on them. It's a well-known fact that if a golfer focuses too much on the bunker and tells themselves that they must not go near it, the chance of actually landing in it increase. Your focus dictates your direction.

It's like saying to a child "don't think of elephants". In order not to think of elephants, you have to actually think of elephants. You must eliminate any negative directions that you give to yourself and to others.

Your statement "don't think of elephants" becomes "think of lions" (or whatever animal you want them to think of).

Focus on the positive results that you want and, once identified and assessed appropriately, don't mention the potential negatives again. Continually worrying about something never actually achieves anything. Think about it once, make the necessary contingencies, and get on with the tasks that you have to do. Don't 'go looking for trouble' as the saying goes.

If you focus on the positives, it will encourage those around you to focus on the positives too.

"There are no secrets to success. It is the result of preparation, hard work, and learning from failure."

- Colin Powell

Staying true to your personal values

I talked earlier about my personal beliefs and, when starting to formulate a plan, a new project, or changes to the way in which you do things, it's important to stay true to your own personal beliefs. If working with other people it's important to incorporate their beliefs too in order to build support and commitment. If you're working within a business, it's also critical to recognise the values of your team or company to ensure that any actions that you take stay true to those values. In that way, you'll give yourself a much better chance of being able to follow through on things that run in parallel with and support your values and beliefs.

Of course, it's relatively simple if your company has a published set of values but most people have never sat down and formally considered what their values are. Here's a list of potential values to stimulate your thought process:

Achievement	Job stability
Advancement and promotion	Knowledge
Adventure	Leadership
Affection	Location
Arts	Loyalty
Being with honest people	Market position
Challenging problems	Meaningful work
Change and variety	Merit
Close relationships	Nature
Community	Order
Competence	Personal Development
Competition	Physical challenge
Cooperation	Pleasure
Country	Power and authority
Creativity	Privacy

Decisiveness	Public service
Democracy	Purity
Ecological awareness	Quality of what I associate with
Economic security	Quality of relationships
Effectiveness	Recognition
Efficiency	Religion
Ethical practice	Reputation
Excellence	Responsibility
Excitement	Security
Fame	Self-respect
Fast living	Serenity
Financial gain	Sophistication
Freedom	Solitude
Friendships	Stability
Growth	Status
Having a family	Supervising others
Helping other people	Time
Honesty	Truth
Independence	Wealth
Inner harmony	Wisdom
Integrity	Working under pressure
Intellectual status	Working with others
Involvement	Working with new people

"Our value is the sum of our values."

- Joe Batten

Stepping outside of your comfort zone

BE BOLD

When you're preparing yourself for this process and you've been reviewing your values, it's time to really take a good look at what you believe in and make sure that it sits comfortably with what you're trying to achieve or where you're trying to go.

For example, if you value 'adventure', 'change', or 'variety', you'll find the process stimulating and easy to progress with. If, on the other hand, you value 'order' and 'stability', you might find it more challenging to break free of your normal 'zone' and move into a space where you might feel uncomfortable.

What you must do is ensure that your need for 'stability' does not get in the way of your need for 'adventure'. You'll need to build in sufficient check-points to give you comfort that all is in order, whilst pushing ahead with new ideas at the same time.

You need to be bold. You need to be certain and you certainly need to think about your desired path in a way that will stretch you. It's unlikely, if not impossible, that you'll be able to change outputs without changing the inputs that you make.

Think about what you're attempting to do. It's certainly not a race but if you're going to change something or achieve something different, you want to do it in the shortest possible time. There is a saying that 'all good things come to those who wait' and to some degree that's true if you look at it from the perspective that patience is a strength. However, you must not let your own 'patience' dictate a softer objective or longer deadline. Yes, by all means be realistic. But don't push back a deadline 'just to be safe'.

If you think you can do it in three months, don't just put in an extra month 'to be safe'. Why can't you achieve it in two months? What's stopping you? Look at what you can control, what you can influence, and what you can do nothing about and focus your energy on where you can make a difference. Don't take the easy route just because you want a quick win. Your 'quick win' could mean extra work in the long term if you've tried to short circuit the process.

Panic Zone

Stretch Zone

Comfort Zone

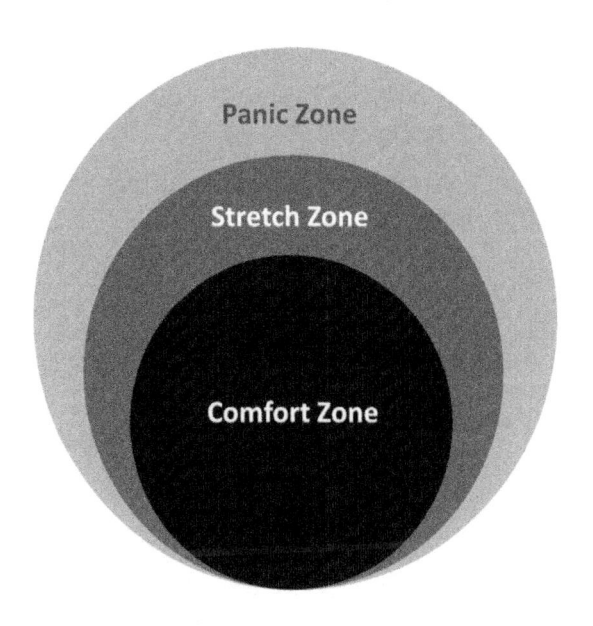

Be bold. Talk to yourself with certainly and set yourself stretching goals. Step out of your 'comfort zone' and into the 'stretch zone'. Set yourself meaningful goals and don't look at things more favourably that you should do just to give yourself an easy time. Also, don't be tempted to set yourself unrealistic goals or try to do too many things. This will simply push you into the 'Panic Zone' and once you arrive in that zone, it's difficult to get out without going right back to square one.

Be precise but be realistic. Stay true to what you're trying to achieve and don't push yourself to the point where the whole process becomes a chore and you simply don't enjoy it. Enjoying the process is an essential component in the overall success that you'll achieve and without enjoyment any progress that you make will seem slow.

You owe it to yourself and those around you who

are also involved in the process. Give this your best shot. Why start something with insufficient energy and motivation to see it through?

Push yourself to burst out of your comfort zone and see what happens.

"When you go out of your comfort zone and it works, there's nothing more satisfying."

- Kristen Wiig

DON'T BE AFRAID TO BE POSITIVE

Most people find it challenging to be overly positive about anything outside of a small number of subjects or items that they feel passionately about. Whilst being overly positive can come across as fanatical or delusional, a lack of positivity never inspired support nor commitment in anyone. Learn to harness your energy and display it appropriately.

For example, if you're trying to persuade the bank manager to support you, then you'll need to appear positive, but also considered and confident. This may be an emotional journey for you, but you need to remain focused and calm. On the other hand, if you're trying to persuade an investor, they need to see that you have been thinking things through and they also need to see your enthusiasm and confidence. They need to see and hear that there is no way that this can fail. They need a plan of course, but they also need passion to convince them. They'll buy into you as much as your idea so bring your confidence to the surface.

It almost goes without saying that if the success of your plan depends upon taking your team with you on the journey, it's critical that they see you as positive and confident. They need to be inspired to follow you. This will mean change for them so embrace them, share your vision, and be positive about the outcomes. Don't hide from the challenges and don't try to claim that it will be an easy transition but give them the reassurance that they need to throw themselves unreservedly behind you.

"Your positive action combined with positive thinking, results in success."

- Shive Khera

IT'S OK TO DAYDREAM

Can you remember as a child, if you were caught staring into space or staring out of the window, you would be accused of being a daydreamer? For some people the observation was that 'you spend so much time daydreaming that you'll never be able to focus on anything' or even worse, 'you'll never amount to anything'.

For many people the concept of daydreaming stays as that – just dreams that they have in the day. So why is it that some individuals can make those dreams become reality? For many people the fear of failure prevents them from taking any action at all. For many the potential problems and pitfalls become the focus not the goal.

You've all heard the sayings that 'success is a journey and not a destination' and 'better to have tried and failed than not to have tried at all'. Both are absolutely true but most of us find it difficult to take the first step to securing our 'dream future'.

Make sure that you 'dream precisely and dread vaguely'. I first heard that phrase several years ago. Why should we place a greater value on our concerns so that it makes us question the quality or practicality of our dreams? By all means plan for contingencies and add some reality into your thoughts, but NEVER let concerns stifle your thoughts and therefore hold back your progress.

For many of us, statements such as 'I want to lose weight' or 'I want to get a better work-life balance' are common place. What we fail to do is to break down what that actually means. No-one can tell you what will work for you. Of course, they can make suggestions, but only you know you.

You know how much discipline you have, how much commitment you have, how much time you have and how badly you want something.

There are no easy answers. There are no short cuts. There are no quick fixes, no easy ways, and certainly no guarantees. However, with careful thought from the outset, you can make life much easier for yourself and give yourself every chance to achieve the success that you want.

"The greatest achievement was at first and for a time, just a dream."

- James Allen

THE 'PERFECT DAY'

Always remember that success is relative and specific to you. Your vision of success must be what drives you. You must not be driven by someone else's view on what success looks like for you. It's important to shake off any restricting thoughts that we might think and we need to challenge any limiting beliefs that we might hold.

It's normal for most people to be very cautious and self-critical when thinking about what they can actually achieve. The possible reasons for failure become actual reasons for failure and, in most cases, stop people from even trying. Remember that we tend to dream 'vaguely' and dread 'precisely'.

The mistake that we often make is that we think that taking time to 'daydream' or to think about what the future might hold should only be done when we have something major to think about in our lives. This is absolutely not the case. Taking time to think things through in an objective, unrestricted way is important whatever the situation or level of the 'goal' is.

Let me give you an example of the type of thinking that I see all of the time. One thing that I often ask the individuals that I work with to do, is to describe what their 'perfect day' would be. On the face of it, a relatively straightforward question. The responses are often straightforward too and I'll hear things like:

"a day at the beach"

"a day's fishing"

"a round of golf with friends"

"time with family"

All perfectly reasonable things to wish for but you'll notice that there are all very vague statements. To put it another way, we're dreaming 'vaguely'.

We need to go back to the original question to challenge ourselves to come up with a better answer. The question that I ask relates to the 'perfect' day for them, not just part of a day.

So, what could they answer? Let's consider the following 'prompt' questions to help us uncover more details that would truly make the day 'perfect':

- Where will you be?
- What time will you get up?
- What will you have for breakfast?
- Who will have breakfast with?
- Where will you go?
- What will you do?
- How will you travel?
- Who will you travel with?
- Where will you have lunch?
- Who will you have lunch with?
- What will you have for lunch?
- Where will you have dinner?
- Who will you have dinner with?
- What will you have for dinner?
- How will you entertain yourself and others?
- Who will you help?
- Will you spend any time working?
- What will you do to make yourself feel happy?
- How will the day end?
- What time will you go to bed?

This is not an exhaustive list, but you'll already see that by simply answering one or two of the questions, you'll be able to put more detail into the description of your 'perfect day'.

When we want to describe something to someone else, we need as much detail as possible so that they precisely understand what we mean. Often, we leave too much information out and expect other people to fill in the gaps. All that happens when we do this is that they fill the gaps with the wrong things and we end up disappointed, frustrated, and even angry. Clearly, this level of thinking requires a different approach, particularly if you're doing it for the first time. We all need time to sit and reflect and, on occasions, we all need time 'away' from our everyday lives and environments.

Working from home, working from a different location, and spending time in the local coffee shop are all good ways to get some new thinking into your life. A different location will provide a different thought stimulus. You see different things and so you can more easily see things differently.

One thing is certain, simply staying in the same location hour after hour, day after day, and week after week is not a good recipe for either thinking creatively about what might be or thinking objectively about what you already have and how you're using it. This doesn't have to be about fundamentally changing what you do – it may just be a way to put a sense of order into what you do so that you can better appreciate it and make the most of it. 'A change is as good as a rest' is how the saying goes but sometimes a rest is as good as a change. Time away from your normal environment or normal activities can be really stimulating.

We've all got friends who holiday in the same place all the time – why do they do that? Sure, you can't go endlessly searching for the perfect holiday, but you should try to vary the holidays and gain more experiences. Is it better to have ten holidays or the same holiday ten times – you decide, but I know what my preference is!

Some people may criticise the fact that I always take my laptop and a note pad away with me on holiday, but I love the thought that I can record thoughts whenever I choose to do so. I love being able to think creatively whenever I want to and being able to commit those thoughts to memory (computer memory). I'll also have a note pad to hand to either write things down or to sketch something which has triggered a thought. Do whatever you prefer to do but don't waste those 'gems' that pop into your head when you're least expecting them.

"Either you run the day, or the day runs you."

- Jim Rohn

Thinking differently – creating the goal

KEY STEPS TO THINKING DIFFERENTLY

Trying to think differently in the same location as you do all of your 'day-to-day' thinking can be challenging. There are times when you need to challenge your normal way of thinking and a change of environment is a simple and effective way of doing this.

"You can't expect to see change if you never do anything differently."

- Meg Biram

As well as 'physical' space, you also need to create space in your mind and that inevitably will mean creating space in your diary. Block out 'quality time' when you can actually break free from the day-to-day routine and think differently about different things. Make it a priority to do this and once it's in the diary, protect this time fiercely.

Invest time to widen your 'frame of reference' and consider what's happening all around you, what the impact will be if you don't change and also what the impact will be on you when you do change.

Learn from what other people are doing but don't just imitate, make it your own and stamp your own identity on it. Observe trends and create a plan that harnesses the positive factors and allows you to manage the challenges.

Challenge your assumptions and build a clear vision of how you want things to be. Be clear what you can control and influence and don't waste energy unnecessarily.

Practice asking: 'What if' and see what answers you get. You may choose to ignore the answers that you do get, but you do so consciously, you haven't forgotten to consider something.

There are a number of techniques that might help:

- Brainstorming (often referred to as 'Ideation')
- Mind Mapping
- Visioning

They will all help you to release new thinking and also allow you to gain valuable input from those around you.

Be careful not to have so many ideas that you become overwhelmed but also make sure that you don't challenge every single idea and comment as this will stop the process in its tracks.

Brainstorming

'Brainstorming' or, as it's more often referred to now, 'Ideation', is the process of gathering as many different ideas about a subject as you possibly can, in as short a time period as possible. Ideas are suggested and noted without comment, reaction, or challenge and individuals are encouraged to think as laterally and as creatively as they can.

The rule is – think first, rationalise, and challenge later. Here are some brief guidelines:

Listen without judging

Let imagination flow freely by withholding judgement on ideas until later. Accept ideas as they are suggested and explore each one with the same level of interest and commitment.

Encourage free thinking

Remove the restrictions of your everyday thinking and challenge yourself and others to come up with unusual and 'wacky' ideas. Move to a different venue to change the physical influences.

Strive for quantity

The more 'oysters' that you have, the more likelihood of finding 'pearls' within them.

Combine ideas and improve them

Look to combine similar ideas together to see if you can further stimulate a different way of thinking – releasing the 'gems' buried deep within your subconscious mind.

Mind Mapping

Very similar to brainstorming is the process of Mind Mapping. This technique involves drawing a diagram with sub headings to provide stimulation to the brain to release ideas and information.

For example, if I asked you to write down as many different types of bird as you could in two minutes, how would you do it? Most people would randomly 'trawl' through the memories and then write down the names of birds as they happened to pop into their heads. You will get some good results, but the process is too 'loose' and you won't be able to capture all the names that are in your memory as you'll struggle to find the key to release the names.

What you need to do is to spend a short while noting the different sub-groups of birds, writing them down and using them to stimulate more in-depth thinking.

You could have:

Birds of prey
Sea birds
Flightless birds
Exotic birds
Wild birds
Domesticated birds

Using each one of these sub-groups, you can now more easily release the names from your mind and, ultimately, you'll end up with a much longer list overall.

Types of Bird – Mind Map example

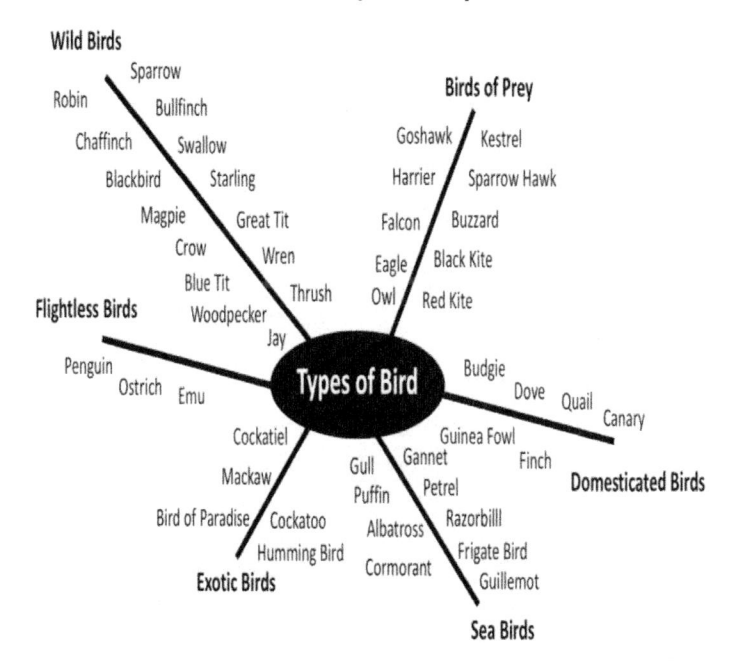

Wild Birds
Sparrow, Robin, Bullfinch, Chaffinch, Swallow, Blackbird, Starling, Magpie, Great Tit, Crow, Wren, Blue Tit, Thrush, Woodpecker, Jay

Birds of Prey
Goshawk, Kestrel, Harrier, Sparrow Hawk, Falcon, Buzzard, Eagle, Black Kite, Owl, Red Kite

Flightless Birds
Penguin, Ostrich, Emu

Domesticated Birds
Budgie, Dove, Quail, Canary, Guinea Fowl, Finch

Exotic Birds
Cockatiel, Mackaw, Bird of Paradise, Cockatoo, Humming Bird

Sea Birds
Gull, Gannet, Puffin, Petrel, Albatross, Razorbill!, Cormorant, Frigate Bird, Guillemot

By using the headings of the 'map' as triggers to release information from the brain, we end up with a list of nearly fifty different types of bird – far more (and far more quickly) than you might get from simply writing them down as they came into your head.

Visioning - Imagining what your success will actually be like

Creating a vision that you can almost 'touch' is a critical part of making the leap towards a new goal and there are two simple ways to approach this using either words or pictures. Being able to sense what your plan will actually feel like when you achieve it is an essential part of building motivation and commitment, both for yourself and for other people.

Using words

One way to do this is to make sure that you write anything down as if it's current and it's already happened. For example, if you say: "we will not work at weekends", it looks like a reasonably positive statement, but it actually sounds very tentative and unsure. Whereas, if you say: "we do not work at weekends", it's a very bold, straightforward statement. It's full of confidence and certainty. It conveys strength and reassures anyone who hears it or reads it that you will actually achieve it.

It's important to speak to yourself and to those around you in a way that both motivates yourself and inspires others to invest in you with their support and guidance. Being able to visualise your goals in a way that makes them so real that you can almost touch them is a critical success factor in making any significant changes. It doesn't guarantee success but it will certainly not adversely affect your progress in any way.

Being successful without being confident is never going to happen and being confident without being arrogant is crucial if you're going to be able to develop and maintain the support of those around you.

Using pictures

Another way to effectively create a 'vision' of what you're trying to achieve is to build a collection of images that represent what your vision of success is.

There are countless images available to you, either in print or online and you are certain to find images that can represent what you are trying to achieve. Set time aside with your spouse or partner to find those key images which clearly demonstrate to anyone who views them, the real extent of what you're trying to achieve.

Being a very 'visual' person, this approach really works for me and I've used it on many occasions inside and outside of work to be able to create and share what my view of success looks like.

It's a very similar approach to that which Interior Designers take when trying to explain how their ideas would actually look in practice. They create a 'mood board' with different samples of paint, wallpaper, cloth, and carpets to allow the customer to actually see and sense what the end result will look like. It's a well-established and extremely effective way of putting your ideas across simply and without ambiguity.

Collecting the images can be fun and there are a huge number of websites available to help you do this. Coming together to review the images with the other people involved is a great way to build motivation, support, and understanding.

It's worth investing the time to be able 'feel' and 'sense' your future success. Having a picture or a series of statements to hand at all times will help to keep you focused and on track as you progress with your plans.

Here's an example of what a vision board might look like if your goal was to take foreign holidays, own a boat or horses, to have a house in the country, and so on.

A personal perspective

I mentioned earlier in the book about the time when I had lost my dream job and found myself at something of a crossroads in my life. When things seemed really challenging and it became difficult to see the way forward, I decided to create my own vision of what I wanted the future to look like and decided to put a plan in place and take actions to achieve my goals.

As this was some time ago, I used magazines as the source of pictures for my 'vision' of success. Clearly today you could use any one of the many photographic libraries online to find exactly the image you were looking for.

It can be much easier to show a picture of what you mean rather than trying to explain it – a picture really can speak a thousand words.

Once you have all the images that you require, arrange them on a table and take time to look at them and enjoy the feelings that you have when you look at them. We need that positive energy to provide the 'fuel' for the journey. Don't assume that just because you have collected a number of pictures together that things will automatically change. Far from it. Without effort and definite actions on your part, nothing will change.

I personally found this process really energising and motivating. Working through it with my wife meant that the vision of the future was a shared perspective and not just some 'pipedream' that only meant something to me. Afterall, you need the support of those around you at some point.

If you're a visual person like me, you'll love this

approach, but whether it's a collection of pictures or a list of items that you have, you have started the journey of shaping your own future.

Edward de Bono's 'Six Thinking Hats'

This concept, created by Edward de Bono, is one of my personal favourite tools for promoting new ideas, freeing up thinking, and bringing clarity to any situation where you have a number of opposing ideas, concepts, and potential doubts to deal with.

Getting the most out of this concept does not actually require you to wear different hats, but it does require you to pay careful attention to the type of thinking you should be doing as dictated by the particular 'hat' that's been nominated at the time.

Without wishing to over-simplify the concept, I've detailed below what each hat stands for and the thinking that it requires from each participant in the process. It may be that all participants think in the same way at the same time or you can even determine who wears which hat based on your knowledge of the individuals concerned.

For example, it is particularly effective to get individuals who are normally upbeat and positive to wear the Black Hat to force them to consider the downside of something. Likewise, it's really useful to get individuals who are normally negative or 'downbeat' in their thinking to wear the Yellow Hat to force them to think positively.

Often when they are forced to think outside of their own comfort zone, individuals come up with some really great contributions that really move the discussions forward.

Mixing the hats up amongst individuals and bringing in different hats at different times will keep the discussions lively and will maintain the energy and focus of all participants. You'll get great results.

The SIX THINKING HATS and required styles of thinking are:

Green Hat

Focuses on creativity – the possibilities of what might be. The Green Hat requires you to allow for free thinking.

Red Hat

Focuses on feelings, hunches, and intuition. The Red Hat requires you to give the emotional view.

Yellow Hat

Symbolises brightness and optimism. The Yellow Hat requires you to think positively.

Black Hat

Plays the 'Devil's Advocate' and focuses on why something might not work. The Black Hat requires you to point out any weaknesses.

White Hat

Deals with facts and figures – quantifiable data.

The White Hat requires you to be neutral and remain objective.

Blue Hat

Manages the thinking process. The Blue Hat focuses on the best use of the hats to get the best result.

I have used this process many times and I've always found that it delivers outstanding results. It works really well in groups where you have diverse opinions and strong beliefs.

A personal perspective

I remember the very first time that I used the 'Six Hats' approach. I was working with a group of senior managers where several individuals had really strong, entrenched beliefs that were limiting their ability to look beyond the current situation. I particularly remember one individual who was extremely stubborn and inflexible, to the point where they were blocking any chance of making progress. I decided to put my trust in the process and bought a number of coloured baseball caps to help with the 'theatre' of what I was trying to do.

The session started as expected with lots of ideas being put forward and individuals 'blocking' those ideas with stubborn refusals to consider anything other than their own, narrow viewpoint. At this point we brought out the hats and explained what we were going to do. There was a great deal of discussion but eventually everyone accepted the approach and the session resumed.

The transformation was incredible. The thought of the 'hats' meant that people felt able to say anything. They could be as positive or as negative as they wanted to. The real turning point was the moment when the really 'negative' person had to wear the 'yellow hat' and be 'positive'. The result was fantastic. They had to set aside their prejudices and force themselves to see a different point of view.

Of course, the situation was repeated when the 'positive' individuals were asked to be 'negative' – they came up with all sorts of things that had not been considered. The fact that they could have such an open discussion was truly liberating. The amount of new thinking that was produced engaged everyone in the group. Every individual felt like they were making a contribution that was being listened to.

At one point the most negative, disruptive person had placed all six hats on their head to make the point that they had totally bought into the process. To see them listening to different ideas and fully participating in the discussion was motivating for everyone else.

It was a fabulous session and it achieved great results for the project and for the team.

I would really recommend that you try it for yourself!

"The mind that opens to a new idea never returns to its original size.'

- Albert Einstein

Potential areas to consider

I mentioned at the start of the book that this approach was not just for business or commercial people. You can use the approach in everyday life too. Let's look at the sort of areas where this approach could work. To help get you started, I've listed the possible first-stage headings for the areas that I mentioned earlier as potential areas where this approach could help:

- Changing jobs
- Moving to a new house
- Losing weight
- Managing relationships
- Taking your business to the next level
- Building a high-performing team

- Managing customers
- Developing new business
- Managing your time more effectively

Please note that these are only suggestions and should be used to stimulate your own thinking. We'll look at one area in more detail later in the book.

Start by pulling together as many ideas for each section as you can. Try to think broadly at first as you can easily re-focus and refine your thoughts later. Avoid trying to debate or to rationalise each idea as you go along as this will only slow the process down and could even stop it. Let your creativity run free and then come back to challenge your thinking.

Changing jobs

Location

Environment

Package/Salary

Hours of working

Career opportunities

Training and development

Being in a job or career that brings enjoyment and fulfilment as well as financial reward is critical for most people. The joy that you get from a high salary will quickly disappear if you become dissatisfied in other key areas and, whilst choosing a job purely based on the salary may seem the right thing to do at a given time in your life, at some point you'll want or need to 're-group' and review what's really important for you to continue in or start a new, sustainable, rewarding, and energising career.

Take time to consider what's really important for you in order to meet your ambitions and fulfil your needs for a balanced lifestyle. Being close to the office and avoiding long commuting times is the dream of many people, whilst for others, working away from home and being able to clearly separate 'work life' from 'home life' is what drives them.

You'll spend around one third of your life 'at work' so it's advisable to give it the consideration it truly deserves.

"Don't pick a job with great vacation time.

Pick a career that doesn't need escaping from."

- Beauti Control

MOVING TO A NEW HOUSE

Financials
Style or type of house
Location and neighbourhood
Local amenities
Friends and family

Moving house can be one of the most stressful things that you will ever do in your life. It's the biggest single investment that most of us will make and there are so many variables that the whole process can seem almost impossible at times and it's often difficult to make sense of all the changes and delays that take place, not to mention the seemingly endless flow of paperwork!

For some people, seeing their dream house and falling in love with it is all it takes to prompt a decision to sell up and move to another house. For others, it can be a simple question of needing to move into the catchment area in order to get the children into a particular school. Whatever the motivation is or how powerful it may be, it's always useful to have a checklist of requirements that allow you to make considered decisions about the suitability of a particular property.

For example, location may not be that important to you at the moment but it could play a critical part when you come to sell the house and need to attract potential buyers.

Whatever your situation, it's worth spending time to identify what's important for you for the short and the long term.

"If we were meant to stay in one place, we'd have roots instead of feet."

- Rachel Wolchin

LOSING WEIGHT

Exercise
Diet
Hobbies and interests
Lifestyle
Career

Safely losing weight and maintaining a healthy weight going forward is something that pre-occupies a great many people. Although it's a significant part, it's not just about what you eat. Other factors will play a major part in helping you to get to your target weight and being able to maintain it.

How much exercise you do and how regularly you do it will play a significant part in any weight loss or control programme. Your choice of career and the subsequent stress that you're under will also be a key contributing factor to your overall health, as will irregular meals and irregular sleep.

There are so many contributing factors, it's vital to spend time thinking through all the alternatives and possibilities.

A PERSONAL PERSPECTIVE

Controlling my weight has always been a challenge for me. The thought of being able to eat just what I want without putting any weight on is probably a dream for many people like me.

I had often wondered how someone who was significantly overweight actually got to that point. After all, you see yourself every day. Surely you can recognise what's happening and do something about it? The truth is very different. You fool yourself into seeing only what you want to see and you kid yourself that one more of something won't matter. The truth is it does.

For me it was a chance meeting with an alternative health practitioner that made the difference for my life. The route of some of the problems that I was experiencing lay in the fact that I was overweight. Solve that problem and the other problems would be easier to deal with.

He made me an offer: do what he told me to do in terms of what I could eat, when I had to eat, how I should breathe, how much sleep I should get, and he would guarantee that I would lose a significant amount of weight.

I really wanted to do it and I really trusted him but my lifestyle at that time made the changes that he asked very difficult. I told him this and I remember him saying then if it's difficult, that's the time to do it. If you really want it, you'll make it happen.

I followed his instructions to the letter and true to form the weight did not come off to start with. However, I had the vision of what I wanted and I knew what I had to do to make it happen. I just had to trust the process. After some weeks I started to notice a difference in how I felt, how I was sleeping, and how my clothes were fitting me. The process was working and it felt great.

Although my weight has increased slightly since I first started the programme as I relaxed my approach to it, I've been able to keep the majority of the weight off and I continue to feel much better about myself and the world around me. It really showed me that if you really want something and you follow the steps to get it, you will surprise yourself at what you can achieve. This was not a fad diet. It was about discipline, willpower, and ambition and, for that reason, it's something that anyone could do.

"A huge part of losing weight is believing you can do it and realising it's not going to happen overnight."

- Inspiremethin/Tumbl

MANAGING RELATIONSHIPS

Communication

Expectations

Time spent with each other

Time spent with family

Hobbies and interests

Social activities

In today's fast-paced, 24/7 world, managing your key relationships is an ongoing challenge. Inside or outside of work, being able to create the right amount of quality time to spend in maintaining or developing relationships is an area that many people spend a great deal of time thinking about.

We spend all of our time at work surrounded by measurement and metrics, we track and measure everything. However, when we get home, we don't track or measure any of the important areas of our lives and it can only be a matter of time before you find yourself in a place where your current relationships aren't working for you. Of course, this can equally apply from a work perspective as it can on a personal basis.

Ignoring what's happening won't solve anything and it's important to get all parties concerned to face up to the reality of what's happening and to work together to create a new picture of what success looks like.

Use the process to think about what's important to all the parties involved and create a template that allows this important part of life to be treated with the time and focus that it deserves.

"Don't build links, build relationships."

- Rand Fishkin

TAKING YOUR BUSINESS TO THE NEXT LEVEL

People and skills
Products and categories
Innovation and development
Customers and trading
Financial
Markets

No matter how successful your business may be, there will come a time when you need to re-evaluate where you are and what you have achieved. You may need to set a new course in order to meet the future needs of the customers or the market.

For ease, I've listed some of the headings in pairs but, depending on your specific business, you may find that each area requires a separate focus.

You may want to take your business into a different area, but have you got the products or indeed the market knowledge to do so? You may have the resources in place, but does your team have the skills required to make the new venture a success?

Being able to clearly communicate what's needed and why it's needed for each area of the business is critical if you are going to be able to effectively move all areas of the business forward at the same speed.

"Some people dream of success whilst other people get up every morning and make it happen."

- Wayne Huizenga

BUILDING A HIGH-PERFORMING TEAM

Vision and goals
Skills and personal attributes
Training and development
Communication
Ground-rules

There are examples of high-performing teams in many different areas. It's particularly easy within the sporting arena to see how an effective team works together and how it achieves the level of success that it does. Our team needs to have the right 'players' and those 'players' need to have a sense of purpose, the right motivation, and the clear direction if they are to fulfil their potential and achieve the goals that you want them to.

It takes time to build a 'winning team' but that can be cut short by taking time to really think in detail about what's required and how it will work on a day-to-day basis.

There needs to be trust amongst all the team members and this can be generated by detailing clear roles and responsibilities and monitoring and sharing progress regularly. Each member of the team needs to know that the other members of the team are doing what they're supposed to be doing. Once you've built that awareness, the individual members can go about their tasks, relaxed in the knowledge that everyone else is getting on with their own tasks.

"If you take out the 'team' in 'teamwork', it's just 'work'. Now, who wants that?"

- Matthew Woodring Stover

MANAGING CUSTOMERS

Depth and breadth of contact
Support team
Skills and development
Customer charter
Relationship management

How you manage your customers has a direct influence on the amount of revenue that they will generate for you. They need to feel valued and need to share the same outlook as you do. Securing their long-term commitment is vital in order to build a sustainable, profitable business.

If you're in business-to-business selling, you need to assess if your customer-facing teams have got the right skills. Are the right people talking to the right people? Do you have regular 'top-to-top' meetings to discuss strategy and share information?

If yours is a business-to-consumer relationship, how are you engaging with them? Are you tracking their feedback and, if so, what are you doing with it?

"Your customer doesn't care how much you know until they know how much you care."

- Damon Richards

DEVELOPING NEW BUSINESS

　Revenue
　Distribution
　Profit
　Products
　Pricing
　Consumers
　Channel or market segment

The first point when thinking about developing new business is to remember that there are only two ways to sell more products: sell more to the customers you have or find more customers. Many businesses chase the new customers without ever fully developing their existing customer base.

Understand where your distribution is currently, particularly your top-twenty products, and identify where you could make gains. Understand what you need to do to attract more consumers to buy your products. Develop a strong digital presence to enable you to communicate with your consumers on a regular basis. Seek feedback, acknowledge that feedback, and act upon it. Track your product reviews and engage in regular two-way dialogue to understand consumer needs and trends.

If you're looking to new markets for your growth, understand what works in your current markets, why it works, and what learnings you can take and apply. Understand the new markets, the different dynamics and do what you need to do to meet the new expectations.

"A satisfied customer is the best business strategy of all."

- Michael LeBoeuf

USING YOUR TIME MORE EFFECTIVELY

Fitness and health
Family and friends
Hobbies and interests
Partner relationships
Home location
Education and personal development
Job and career

How often have you heard people talk about finding the perfect 'work- life' balance? For some, it seems an endless struggle, whilst for others they seem to have things well sorted out. How can this be? What do they do to make things run so smoothly?

The good thing is that there's no real magic involved. Just a simple understanding of what's important and scheduling those things in the diary and letting other things fit in around them.

It's about setting realistic expectations and working to them. Don't promise to be home on time every night when you know that you'll never be able to deliver on that commitment.

Have you ever noticed how some people carry their 'To Do' list around with them like a badge of honour? They make a point of using it to show you how busy they are but, as we all know, being busy is not the same as being effective. They seem to 'wallow' in their own frustration and seem unable to find a way out of it.

"Action expresses priorities."

- Mahatma Gandhi

A PERSONAL PERSPECTIVE

For a great many people, managing time is a real challenge and one that always seems to get the better of them. We all have the same amount of time available, but some people seem more in control of their time than we do of ours.

In reality, we all get times when events seem to control us and we appear to have too many tasks to do within the time that we have available. This is particularly true when starting a new business. You have to plan your time, but you have to remain flexible to be able to accommodate new leads and potential new business.

When I started my business, I was looking forward to being totally flexible with how I spent my time but I quickly realised that without some sort of discipline, you can quickly get behind with tasks that you need to complete.

I learned that by allocating certain times of the day and the week to complete key tasks, I can much better organise my time. I get the key tasks done and still give myself time to be flexible when I need to. Some of the key tasks are 'need to do' rather than 'nice to do'. They're the sort of tasks that other people do for you when you work in a corporate environment, but you quickly realise that if you get behind with them (such as invoicing), you quickly run into problems!

I run my diary like a school timetable and build times in to complete key tasks. Whilst some are a pleasure, some are a real chore (a bit like Physics felt like when I was at school!) but by allocating the time in the diary, I can get through the 'dull' stuff because I know that the exciting stuff is still to come.

Value your time – if you don't, no one else will!

Creating your plan

Let's start to look in more detail at one area that we've already mentioned by way of an example of how to approach the challenge and what the outputs might look like.

"Plans are nothing.
Planning is everything."

- Dwight D Eisenhower

In truth, anyone can write a plan. Simply writing something down without any thoughts as to how those plans might be achieved makes no sense at all. Investing quality time in thinking, working through options, and scheduling activities will pay dividends in the long term. It's about balance. Don't take too long planning that you don't get started, but don't launch into taking actions so quickly that you have to undo what you've already done and you are constantly having to make adjustments and changes.

The plan needs to follow a simple format:

Step 1 - Plan

Step 2 - Do

Step 3 - Review

Invest time in the planning at the beginning of the process and don't burden yourself with having to make changes or take actions too quickly. This is not a race. It's about taking simple actions in order to reach your desired goal.

POSITIVE WORDS

Although most of our communication 'impact' comes from our body language, the words that we choose are also important. Why make life difficult for yourself by choosing 'neutral' words and having to work really hard to increase their impact with positive expressions and gestures.

Start by choosing positive words right from the outset. Imagine how much easier it will be to make the overall message positive and motivating.

To simplify your job of thinking of the right words to use, I've listed below a selection of positive words that you could consider using when writing your vision, your plan, or simply in everyday conversation.

Remember, using positive words is just the start. Be sure to focus on the tone of voice that you use and the gestures that you display. If you're not sincere and honest in what you're saying and how you're saying it, it will show through.

Also, remember that no matter how much you 'dress up' an unclear, poorly considered, non-specific message, no amount of positive words just thrown in without proper thought will ever be a substitute for clarity, passion, and sincerity.

A	B	C
absolutely	beautiful	celebrated
acclaimed	believe	champion
accomplishment	bountiful	constant
achievement	broad	cool
action	brilliant	courageous
adventure	bubbly	creative
agree		
amazing		
awesome		

D	E	F
dazzling	easy	fabulous
delightful	effective	fair
determined	efficient	familiar
distinguished	effortless	fantastic
dominant	encouraging	free
	endorsed	fresh
	energized	friendly
	engaging	fun
	enthusiastic	
	essential	
	ethical	
	excellent	
	exciting	

G	H	I
genuine	happy	ideal
good	harmony	impressive
great	healing	independent
green	health	innovative
grow	honest	instant intuitive
	honourable	inventive

J	K	L
joy	keen	laugh
jolly	kind	legendary
	knowledgeable	light
		longevity
		luck
		lucky

M	N	O
marvellous	natural	open
masterful	novel	opportunity
meaningful	now	optimistic
motivating	nutritious	
moving		

P	Q	R
perfect	qualified	ready
phenomenal	quality	reassuring
plentiful	quick	refreshing
popular		reliable
positive		remarkable
powerful		resolute
prepared		respected
principled		rewarding
productive		right
progress		robust
protect		
proud		

S	T	U
safe	terrific	unreal
secure	thorough	up
simple	thrilling	upbeat
skilful	thriving	
special	transform	
spirited	transformational	
stunning	transformative	
success	trust	
superb	trusted	
support	truth	
surprise		

V	W	Y
valued	wealth	Yes
vibrant	welcome	
vital	well	Z
	whole	Zeal
	wonderful	
	worthy	
	wow	

WHO SHOULD YOU SHARE YOUR PLANS WITH?

It's essential to involve other people in this process to ensure their future buy in and support – you never know when you may need it. You need to be certain that the people that you share your thoughts with are going to challenge you but are not going to be so negative in their feedback that they disrespect your thinking and ultimately discourage you from taking action.

It's a fact that not everyone will see things your way and you will certainly be challenged. Whether it's your spouse, your business partner, a friend, or a member of your own family, it's important to choose people who have proven themselves to you as being objective and considered. It may be that the first person that you choose to share anything with is an acquaintance rather than a close friend or member of your own family. Getting feedback from someone who has no immediate connection with you can provide totally objective feedback. They're seeing things for the first time and reacting in an honest and unbiased way that allows you to review your thinking and make any necessary changes to your objectives or plans.

Let me share a short anecdote with you.

Back when I was working as a trainer, I worked with individuals from all levels and disciplines of business. They all had one thing in common. When faced with a new idea or concept, their initial reaction was not one of 'exploration' but was usually one of 'denial'. Their initial comment was often: "That's all very well, but it won't always work, will it?"

Of course, they were absolutely correct. There aren't many things that will give consistent results, no matter who does them or when they do them. However, that's not the point. The key thing to realise is that 'won't always' means 'will sometimes'. You just need to broaden your thinking and try new things. If they don't work, you can always go back to the ways in which you did things before. You've lost nothing – aside from a bit of time, maybe.

But what if they do work? How much better could your daily experiences be? If you go through your life in 'denial' you'll never know how good things might have been. You will have lost the opportunity to explore and to grow.

When you're considering who to involve in the process and who to share your plans with, try to choose individuals who you can also involve in your brainstorming and creative thinking sessions. Choose people whom you can depend upon to be open, honest, and free-thinking, and whose opinion you value.

"The more we share,

the more we have."

- Leonard Nimoy

Working through the process

Following the process is key to making progress. There are no short cuts to get to your end goal but there are quick wins to be made which will create momentum and will encourage you and those around you to continue to put the effort into achieving your end goal.

Planning small, achievable steps is critical if you are to make progress quickly and consistently. Of course, it's not a race but any delays in the process will cause you unrest and could, if they go unchecked, put an end to the whole process.

What I'd like to do in the chapter is to work through one of our early examples in more detail to show you the type of thinking and planning that should take place. The process is very simple but that does not mean that we should not give each stage our full attention and create a meaningful goal and an achievable action plan. Remember that we need to be realistic but that certainly doesn't mean that we shouldn't stretch ourselves. How much 'stretch' you feel comfortable with is entirely your choice but too much 'stretch' might slow your progress and you need to maintain effort and pace throughout the process.

"Trust the process. Your time is coming. Just do the work and the results will handle themselves."

- Tony Gaskins

The process is in four distinct phases:

1. Defining 'what does success look like?'
2. Establishing where are we now
3. Detailing the specific actions needed to reach the plan
4. Monitoring and measuring progress

The goal
What does success look like?

⬇

Present situation
Where are you now?

⬇

Action Plan
What needs to happen?

⬇

Progress update
What's been achieved?

Let's look at each stage in more detail, and for this I'm going to use an example from earlier – **managing your time more effectively.**

The potential areas to look at that we identified are:

  Fitness and health
  Family and friends
  Hobbies and interests
  Partner relationships
  Home and location
  Education and personal development
  Job and career

Let's look at each area in more detail and some ideas that we could include. Remember, this is only an example and should not be used as a 'live' example by you. It's important that your content is exactly that – your content. Take ideas from other sources but always make sure that your vision of success is personal to you and therefore any actions that you take will be and must be personal to you. Write the actions in the present tense – assume that you're already doing them. This makes them come alive and seem 'real' to you.

WHAT DOES SUCCESS LOOK LIKE?

For each area that we have defined, let's look at the statements that effectively and accurately express what success looks like for us:

  Fitness and health
  Family and friends
  Hobbies and interests
  Partner relationships
  Home and location
  Education and personal development
  Job and career

For each of focus, let's look at the possibilities that we might see as potential successes. All should be stretching but not so difficult as to prevent us from even starting. Recognise that you're expressing the 'destination at this stage', not the journey.

FITNESS AND HEATH

I walk 10,000 steps per day
I cycle once per week
I drink alcohol only at weekends
I weigh 14 stones/89 kilos
I go to bed at 10.00 p.m.
I drink tea/coffee only at weekends
I visit the gym on two days per week

FAMILY AND FRIENDS

I visit my parents once per month
I speak to my siblings once per week
I see my close friends at weekends
We have family meal times
I meet with all my family twice a year
I holiday with friends once per year

HOBBIES AND INTERESTS

I play tennis once per week
I paint at weekends
I visit an antique fair every month
I read every day

I belong to a local dramatic group
I am a member of the school council

HOME AND LOCATION

We share all household chores
Our home is a joint project
We have a designated 'quiet' area
We spend 1/2 days a week gardening
We grow our own vegetables
We have a cleaner

EDUCATION AND PERSONAL DEVELOPMENT

I am knowledgeable about antiques
I read one novel per month
I speak French
I am studying for my degree
I am a volunteer counsellor
I coach my local football team

JOB AND CAREER

I love my job
I leave work on time twice per week
I don't stay away from home
My office is 30 minutes from home
I work flexi-time
I manage a department

You'll notice two things about the detailed statements within each section:

1. They're written in the present tense
2. There are some things that are relatively quick wins

It's important to write the objectives down in the present tense and it gives them energy and makes them look and feel 'real'. For example: "I leave work on time twice per week" is a much more positive and confident statement than "I will leave work on time twice per week" which just sounds like wishful thinking. It's also important to have some objectives that are relatively easy to achieve as these can be your quick wins. For example: "We have a designated quiet area" is something that you can do immediately and so you can progress with one element very easily.

Once you've identified what your view of success looks like and you've either shared it or agreed it with your partner, colleagues, or friends, it's time to move to the next stage which is understanding where you are against each of the statements and therefore begin the process of planning the actions that need to be taken to get you where you want to be.

Remember, these statements all represent the 'end game', the 'destination'. Once you've established what the gap is between where you want to be and where you are now, you can start to plan the journey in such a way that it allows you to reach the destination in the optimum time period.

For ease, I've provided 'Template A' at the back of the book to get you started and give you a framework.

ESTABLISHING WHERE WE ARE NOW

Starting the process by stating where you want to be (the 'end game') and then assessing where you are, you allow your mind to run freely and think creatively, unhampered by the constraints of what exists at the moment. Your thinking is less restricted than it might ordinarily be.

Once you've identified what success looks like, shared it, and agreed the outcomes with all stakeholders (family, friends, or colleagues), you're ready to move to the next stage of the process and assess where you are now. Using a scale from 1 to 10, assess your current position against where you want to be as expressed in your goal statement. '1' indicating that you're a long way from your goal and '10' indicating that you're already there!

For example, if your goal states that you walk 10,000 steps per day and you only walk 2,000 steps, you rate yourself with a score of '2'. If your goal says that you go to bed at 10.00 p.m. on two nights and you only do this one night, you rate yourself '5', and so on.

If you're setting yourself all these new things to do and you still want to play tennis once per week, then rate yourself as a '10' against that goal and make sure that you build it into your schedule.

As stated earlier in the book, it's important to look for 'quick wins' and these will build confidence and momentum. Not everything can be a 'quick win' but it's important to establish a balance of simple vs complex or challenging actions. For example, take the statement 'we have a designated quiet area in the house'. If you don't have such an area, it's a very simple and quick step to designate an area, thereby achieving a very quick win.

Some statements will simply be a case of 'I don't do it and now I do', whereas some will require much more work and planning. Goals such as 'speaking French' and 'being a volunteer counsellor' are not quick wins by any means and will require a degree of research and application if you are to achieve them within the required timescale.

TIMESCALE

It's vital when undertaking something like this to give yourself enough time to fully achieve what you set out to achieve. These are not likely to be short-term projects and so will require planning and commitment to make them happen.

Simply writing them down doesn't move you forward but the clarity that comes from the goals being simply and clearly expressed will enable you to share your objectives, to gain support from those around you and to be able to monitor your progress as you go along.

Don't be a slave to the timescale that you've set. Allow yourself time to explore new areas properly. Don't rush. Take your time and enjoy the fact that your destination is clearly mapped out.

"Time is free, but it's priceless You can't own it, but you can use it.

You can't keep it, but you can spend it.

Once you've lost it, You can never get it back."

- Harvey Mackay

FITNESS AND HEATH   **RATING**

I walk 10,000 steps per day	
I cycle once per week	
I drink alcohol only at weekends	
I weigh 14 stones/89 kilos	
I go to bed at 10.00 p.m. on two nights	
I drink tea/coffee only at weekends	
I visit the gym two days per week	

FAMILY AND FRIENDS   **RATING**

I visit my parents once per month	
I speak to my siblings once per week	
I see my close friends at weekends	
We have family meal times	
I meet with all my family twice a year	
I holiday with friends once per year	

HOBBIES AND INTERESTS   **RATING**

I play tennis once per week	
I paint at weekends	
I visit an antique fair every month	
I read every day	
I belong to a local dramatic group	
I am a member of the school council	

PARTNER RELATIONSHIPS   **RATING**

I keep one night a week free for us	
We have a date night every month	
I make time to listen to him/her	
I am interested in his/her family	
We spend time cooking together	

We do not have any secrets	

HOME AND LOCATION   **RATING**

We share all household chores	
Our home is a joint project	
We have a designated 'quiet' area	
I spend 1/2 days a week gardening	
We grow our own vegetables	
We have a cleaner	

EDUCATION AND PERSONAL DEVELOPMENT   **RATING**

I am knowledgeable about antiques	
I read one novel per month	
I speak French	
I am studying for my degree	
I am a volunteer counsellor	
I coach my local football team	

JOB AND CAREER   **RATING**

I love my job	
I leave work on time twice per week	
I don't stay away from home	
My office is 30 minutes from home	
I work flexi-time	
I manage a department	

Use the scale from 1 to 10 as detailed or alternatively, use the traffic light system for a very visual way of seeing your progress:

Red   Not started

Orange   In progress

Green   Achieved

Use whatever suits you and makes it easy for to measure your progress.

Detailing specific actions

Once you've set your goal and established where you are against each of the elements, it's time to break out the detailed actions that will get you from where you are to where you want to be.

Let's look at one area and see what the actions might be based on the scoring that I've indicated:

Hobbies and Interests   Rating

I play tennis once per week	1
I paint at weekends	1
I visit an antique fair every month	4

I read every day	4
I belong to a local dramatic group	1
I am a member of the school council	1

It's clear looking at my assessment, that I've got quite a bit of work to do. So, how do I start? Take the statement 'I play tennis every week'. My assessment score indicates that currently I'm not doing that and so I need to look at the actions that I need to take.

I used to play when I was younger, I've had the idea of taking the sport up again for a long time. I've noticed that there is a local tennis club and that the local sports centre also has several public courts that I could use. However, my tennis racquet is old, I'll need to purchase a new one if I'm not going to look out of place. I'll also need some new kit (of course!). My list of actions might be something like this:

1 Research all potential mid-price tennis racquets
2 Purchase new tennis racquet
3 Find out about the cost of membership at a local tennis club
4 Ask friends and family if they know anyone who is a member
5 Find out how much it costs to play at the local sports centre
6 Research options for kit
7 Purchase kit based on decision re club or sports centre

I need to set a time by which I would like to start playing tennis again and therefore need to complete all the tasks. If I choose to give myself four weeks, it allows me time to do my own research and to talk to friends and family. I can make a decision about joining the club or playing at the local sports centre without feeling rushed. If I choose the sports centre, I can always review at a later date whether or not to join the club.

For some people, committing to a membership is the way in which they motivate themselves to start and to continue with something new. For others, they prefer to take it one step at a time and review as they go. Again, it's a personal choice so do what feels right for you.

If you're used to writing things down, then you'll find the planning process pretty straightforward. For those of you who are not so used to writing down objectives and plans, there's a simple template on page 143 to help get you started.

This may seem as if you're creating a lot of work and actually if it seems like a lot of work, you're probably not going to stick at whatever it is you decided to change. There are no gains to be made without effort. Nothing comes to those who do nothing. Investing time in the planning will pay dividends in the future. Of course, you might get lucky, but you can't plan everything on luck. Luck is exactly what it says it is; lucky. That also means that it is unpredictable – you can't plan your future in this way.

Monitoring and measuring progress

It's critical to the success of your overall plan that you check and measure progress regularly. If you're going off course, it's important to realise this as soon as possible to ensure that any corrective action required is minimal. I've always used the example of an airplane journey as a way of showing how important it is to have a plan, share the plan, use the plan, monitor your progress, and make adjustments as you go. Let me explain.

It's a well-known fact that aircraft fly off course for a large proportion of the time that they are in the air. In some instances, this can be for as much as 50% of the flight time. So, how does the crew ensure that the flight arrives at the correct destination at the correct time? The purpose and role of the pilot and the systems on board is to continually bring the plane back on course so that it arrives on schedule at its destination. There is a start point and a destination. There is a flight plan. All three things are known to everyone involved in making that journey happen safely – the Air Crew and Air Traffic Control. The Air Crew need the flight plan to know which headings to follow, what speed to fly and what adjustments to make. Air Traffic Control need the flight plan to know where the plane should be, where it is and what progress it's making. If something happens en-route, there's always someone who will pick it up and communicate what's happened. It's also worth remembering that there is always more than one plane in the sky at any one time. It's pretty important to be able to see all the flight plans to make sure that no two aircraft are trying to use the same air space at the same time.

In life, you are the 'pilot' of your own craft. To reach your goals, your destination of health, happiness, prosperity, a good life or whatever it might be, you must do as a pilot does. You must first of all determine your destination. This requires clear, specific goals, written down, with plans to accomplish them for each day. It's critical to share that plan with someone close to you, someone that you can trust. You're not looking for permission, you're looking for help and support along the way. Also, depending on whom you share the plans with, you might find out about someone else in your 'air space' and you can take the necessary actions to avoid a 'collision'.

Secondly, you must be prepared to take-off toward your destination with no guarantee of success. You must be willing to move out of your comfort zone and take risks continually, even though you know that most of them will not succeed, at least at the beginning.

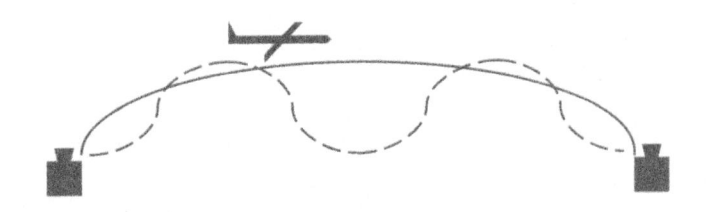

Working on the assumption that, like the aircraft, you could also be off course for as much as 50% of the time, the third part and the real secret of success is that you must be prepared to make continual course corrections. Just as an aircraft faces headwinds, downdrafts, storm fronts, wind shear, lightning and unexpected turbulence, you will experience the same in the pursuit of any worthwhile goal.

The key to success is for you to keep your mind fixed clearly on the goal and to remain flexible about the ways in which you can achieve them. Be open to new ideas and inputs from different sources. Learn from every experience that you have. Look for the good in any challenge, setback, or difficulty.

Most of all, you must commit in advance that you will never give up. Your ability to persist in the face of all adversity in the direction of your goals is what will ultimately bring you success.

"Success is falling nine times and getting up ten."

- Jon Bon Jovi

STAYING FOCUSED AND MOTIVATED

It's critical to the achievement of your key objectives that you stay focused and motivated to carry on. There will be time when the path will be difficult and you will get frustrated, but you need to remain as enthusiastic and committed as you did when you set out on the journey.

Going back to the example of the aircraft, the one thing that most airlines do is to add a time 'buffer' into their timetable by over-estimating the time that each journey will take.

For example, the normal timetable for most leading UK airlines will show the flight time from Heathrow to Glasgow as ninety minutes. This is around thirty minutes longer than the journey actually takes and therefore they have built in a 'buffer' to allow for weather, terminal delays and airport congestion. If you're familiar with one particular Irish airline, they always play a fanfare upon landing proclaiming their early arrival. They set their goal and give themselves every chance of consistently achieving it.

We can also use this approach for our own personal advantage. Finishing earlier than we planned is a great motivating factor and, if we build in a 'tolerance' within our plans, we give ourselves every chance of finishing ahead of schedule. This is particularly important when you have other parties interested in your progress – investors, banks etc.

We should also commit to check our progress at regular and frequent intervals. Not so frequent that we won't actually be able to show any progress but not so long that we could be way off course or behind schedule before we realise. Staying on track is a great motivator and even if you are slightly adrift from your planned position, the fact that you've recognised that in good time means that you can take great comfort in the fact that any adjustments that you may have to make are very small and relatively straightforward to carry out.

Make no mistake, the path can and will get lonely at times. You will have doubts along the way and you will question your intentions. Staying focused and motivated will be critical to your success. Being able to secure 'quick wins' will boost your motivation and confidence. Take advantage of these situations as 'fuel' to fire your overall project.

"Believe in yourself! Have faith in your abilities! Without a humble but reasonable confidence in your own powers you cannot be successful or happy."

- Norman Vincent Peale

Enjoying success

As I said right at the start of the book, this is not a 'get-rich-quick' scheme, there are no guarantees and it's certainly not about showing you a shortcut to get where you want to be. If you've followed the process as outlined, you will have put a great deal of effort into the process and you deserve to enjoy your success when you get there.

There will come a time when you reach the time limit that you set at the beginning of your journey and, whilst you could extend it, it's worth taking time to reflect on what you've actually achieved. Don't focus on the few things that may not have happened. You will have made significant progress.

One of my favourite sayings that's become one of the key principles in my life is:

"Never let perfect be the enemy of good."

In other words, what you've achieved may not match every expectation that you had but you will have made significant progress. You might not have lost as much weight as you planned to, but you've still lost a significant amount of weight. You might not be working in the job role that you aspire to but you've made progress towards it.

Success is what you think it is. It's not what is portrayed every day in the media. Be proud of what you have achieved and take time to celebrate success with those who have helped you.

All of us need to step out of our comfort zones at some point in our lives. Most people run back into them the minute that they step outside because they fear what might happen. They're not willing to take the risk to see how far that they can push themselves and to see how much they can achieve.

You have to ask yourself what is the worst thing that can happen if you start on this process. What if you fail? Well, you just go back to what you were doing before. You've lost nothing.

But what if you succeed? The feelings of achievement and self-belief will be fantastic and you'll have proven the 'doubters' wrong and demonstrated that you can do something different and you can achieve great things for you and your family.

I truly believe that life is there for the taking. It's what we make it and shouldn't be just what happens to us. Take the chance, grab the opportunity, and see where you can go. See exactly what success looks like for you.

SUMMARY

One of the biggest steps forward that you can make is to realise that you can build your own vision of success. You don't have to live your life constantly comparing yourself to someone else's view of what good looks like. You don't have to be a slave to media images of success.

By taking time to build a clear picture, one that's easy to communicate and to explain to others, you'll give yourself a structure, a plan to follow to enable you to deliver what success looks like for you.

Not everything will work first time but stick at it. You made the commitment to try and you owe it to yourself to give it your best shot. Whatever you decide to do, whatever plans you make, you need to remember that it's not a race. You set the time limits, you set the pace. Be honest with yourself and others right from the start and don't be tempted to make over-ambitious promises that sound great at the time but will only come back to drag you down later.

By setting realistic goals and simple steps towards those goals, you'll give yourself every chance of being successful at what you do. Celebrate success at every opportunity as the path will get tough and you will be challenged.

Good luck in everything that you do.

Useful Tools

TEMPLATE A

Focus Areas	Detail	Current status

Template B

Goal	Action	Timing	Status

ABOUT THE 496 PARTNERSHIP

The 496 Partnership was born out of my experience that properly motivated individuals can achieve great things. Too often, individual talent is underused and underdeveloped because of a lack of focus and support. My approach is one-on-one, 'partnering' with talented individuals and working with them to help them achieve their maximum potential. Very much 'just in time' rather than 'just in case'.

It's a partnership because not only do I get to work in a close and very focused way with individuals, but I also work with a team of experienced, practical, and highly motivated business professionals who share my beliefs and goals. My passion is 'Making People Count'.

WHY 496?

496 is a 'perfect number' – it's divisible by: 1, 2, 4, 8, 16, 31, 62, 124, and 248. If you take all of those individual component numbers and add them together, the total comes to 496. Just as the number 496 is made up of multiples of smaller numbers, organisations also consist of many different

components – departments, teams, and individuals. Indeed, our own lives have many different 'components' that shape who and what we are.

With any one of the numbers missing, any components missing, or any members of the team not performing, we cannot get to 100%. Likewise, in our own lives we often hear the phrase, "I'm not feeling 100%". We know that it doesn't mean that everything is wrong. It simply means that one aspect of our day-to-day lives is causing us concern.

WANT TO BRING THIS TO LIFE IN YOUR BUSINESS?

If you feel energised and inspired by what you've read but feel that you'd like assistance to bring it to life within your business, why not get in touch and talk through how I can work with you and your team to run an individual session, tailored for you and your business.

This could be either an individual or a team session that will take you through the process from start to finish, ensuring that you get full buy in and support at every stage and agreeing action plans to make sure that the necessary changes are made and embedded within your business.

Get in touch for a no-obligation discussion and let me know exactly what you're trying to achieve. I'd be delighted to discuss your specific requirements and where I can help you.

vance@496partnership.com

About the Author

Vance Withers was born in the county of Somerset in the United Kingdom and is an experienced, passionate commercial leader with over forty years of international sales and management experience.

His passion for developing people started early on in his career when he secured the position of National Sales Trainer and, having established the procedures and systems for developing the sales team, he moved into his first team management role at the age of twenty-three. He quickly established a reputation for supporting and developing people, as well as achieving outstanding business results. He worked for a number of years as a management consultant, before returning to an international commercial role.

He started the 496 Partnership in 2017 to allow him to get back to his passion for helping individuals and businesses to achieve their full potential.

He is an accomplished musician and chef, a keen collector of antiques, and an enthusiastic mountain biker and boater.

He currently lives in the village of Birtsmorton, Worcestershire, with his wife Karen.